Hawai'i Cooks

with

SPAM®

Hawai'i Cooks
with
SPAM®

Local Recipes Featuring
Our Favorite Canned Meat

Muriel Miura

Food Styling by Hideaki Miyoshi
Photography by Kaz Tanabe

Mutual Publishing

Dedication

To all who enjoy SPAM®,
and especially to my grandchildren,
Alissa and Stephen,
who enjoy having regular servings of
SPAM®.

Copyright © 2008 by Mutual Publishing

The information contained in this book is accurate and complete to the best of our knowledge. All recipes and recommendations are made without guarantees. The author and publisher disclaim all liabilities in connection with the use of the information contain within.

SPAM® is a registered trademark of Hormel Foods, LLC and is being used with permission from Hormel Foods.

Library of Congress Cataloging-in-Publication Data

Miura, Muriel.
  Hawai'i cooks with spam : local recipes featuring our favorite canned meat / Muriel Miura ; food styling by Hideaki Miyoshi ; photography by Kaz Tanabe.
     p. cm.
  Includes index.
  ISBN 1-56647-853-7 (softcover wire-o bound : alk. paper)
  1. Cookery (Meat) 2. Cookery (Canned foods) 3. Spam (Trademark) 4. Canned meat. 5. Cookery--Hawaii. I. Title.
  TX749.M555 2008
  641.3'6--dc22
          2007050419

ISBN-10: 1-56647-853-7
ISBN-13: 978-1-56647-853-3
Design by Courtney Young
Seventh Printing, April 2017

Mutual Publishing, LLC
1215 Center Street, Suite 210
Honolulu, Hawai'i 96816
Ph: 808-732-1709 / Fax: 808-734-4094
email: info@mutualpublishing.com
www.mutualpublishing.com

Printed in Korea

Table of Contents

Preface

Of all my books, *Hawai'i Cooks with SPAM®* has been the most spontaneous. In compiling the recipes for this book to celebrate the seventieth anniversary of SPAM®, I found that most folks in Hawai'i consider SPAM® a delicious treat. Hawai'i consumes more than six million cans per year, or six cans per person per year—the most in the United States. Of course, there are those who turn a cold shoulder to SPAM®, but they are few and far between. Besides, who could dispute the popularity of SPAM®?

People in Hawai'i are passionate about SPAM®, creatively combining it with just about anything. Underscoring the diversity of SPAM®, you'll find that SPAM™ ideas influenced by Hawai'i's rich ethnic heritage, accented with spices and flavors of many lands, abound in this collection. Here is a generous sampling of SPAM™ favorites with an international flavor. Many of the recipes will evoke warm memories, stimulate you to create your own, or reconnect you with fondly remembered dishes that signify the joy of gathering to eat with family and friends.

Miss SPAM®? Get SPAM® back into your life through the pages of *Hawai'i Cooks with SPAM®*, a well-illustrated, colorful, fun, and user-friendly cookbook. You'll re-discover the savory flavor of SPAM®. You'll definitely love the convenience of SPAM® and enjoy its numerous varieties. SPAM® is delicious and versatile, as the recipes will demonstrate.

Muriel Miura

Muriel Miura, CCFS

Acknowledgments

My heartfelt thanks to a remarkable number of people who assisted in the production of this book—people who have been working with me from the beginning to the end.

Special thanks to my husband, Yoshi, and my daughter, Shari, and her family—her husband, Geoff, and children, Alissa and Stephen—for their never-ending encouragement and support.

Family, friends, and fans who generously shared their favorite recipes.

Hoagy Gamble of L. H. Gamble Company for support and contributions.

Hormel Foods for permitting the use of their SPAM trademark and all SPAM® derived terms in this book.

Hideaki Miyoshi, with assistance from Gay Wong, for food preparation and styling; Kaz Tanabe for photography; and Jane Gillespie for art direction.

And sincerest thanks to everyone at Mutual Publishing for their spirit, style, talent, and energy—especially Bennett Hymer who saw us through it all.

Introduction

SPAM®, a family of tasty and pre-cooked luncheon meats, is a product of Hormel Foods Corporation (formerly Hormel & Company). Eleven years after introducing the first canned ham in 1926, Jay C. Hormel, son of the company's founder, determined to find a use for surplus pork shoulder, developed a distinctive canned blend of chopped pork known as HORMEL® spiced ham that didn't require refrigeration. The Austin, Minnesota-based Hormel Company sponsored a contest to find a name that was unique to this new product and the winning entry, SPAM®, was submitted by Kenneth Daigneau, an actor from New York and brother of a Hormel vice present. He won $100 for naming this great tasting, convenient, and moderately priced luncheon meat.

Through more than seven decades, SPAM® has remained Hawai'i's favorite canned meat. It is a contemporary product known for its versatility, quality, great taste, and convenience. The SPAM® Family of Products are fully cooked, ready-to-eat, and have a good shelf life. They are used to flavor many dishes and are delicious with rice, noodles, and vegetables— and especially great for musubi and Island-style plate lunches!

Many of these recipes are treasured ones from friends, family, and fans. They are all the result of years of sharing the fun of cooking. You'll find that there is no limit to food horizons with SPAM®. Use these recipes as a guide to create some of your own, and enjoy. Whatever the reason or season, *Hawai'i Cooks with SPAM®* will help you provide the perfect dish—simple or fancy—for any meal or occasion. Let's eat SPAM®!

I. SPAM-A-RAZZI™
All About SPAM®

About SPAM® Classic

Hailed as the "miracle meat," SPAM® attracted the attention of the United States military during World War II for its shelf-stable attributes, and by 1940 most Americans overseas had gotten a taste of it. Our allies were enjoying SPAM® soon after. Since fresh meat was difficult to get, surpluses of SPAM® from the soldiers made their way into Hawai'i's diets as well as those of other Pacific islands...the rest is history. SPAM® remains a part of Hawai'i's culture today, and Hawai'i is the leading consumer of SPAM® in the United States with more than six milliion cans per year, or six cans per person per year consumed. According to Hormel Foods, more than six billion cans of SPAM® were produced by 2002. Amazing, isn't it?

Because of its versatility and unique flavor, SPAM® is used in a variety of ways, such as sandwich meats, salad ingredients, sushi filling, musubi toppings, or to make a meaty macaroni and cheese. It is served or cooked with cheese, eggs, pineapples; it is sliced, diced, chopped, grated. Hot or cold, baked or fried—the combinations are endless. In keeping with Hawai'i's tradition of ethnic foods, the recipes in this book reflect the cultural influences of various countries.

Nutrition Facts*

Nutrition Facts for SPAM® 25% Less Sodium:
Serving Size: 2 oz. (56 g)
Servings per Container: 6
Calories: 180
Fat Calories: 140

Amount/serving	%DV*	Amount/serving	%DV*
Total Fat 16 g	25%	Total Carb. 1 g	0%
Sat. Fat 6 g	30%	Fiber 0 g	0%
Cholest. 40 mg	13%	Sugars 0 g	0%
Sodium 580 mg	24%	Protein 7 g	
Vitamin A	0%	Vitamin C	30%
Calcium	0%	Iron	2%

*Percent Daily Values (DV) based on 2,000-calorie diet. Nutritional data subject to change based on type of SPAM®; data available on each can.

SPAM® Family of Products

The labeled ingredients in the Classic (original) variety of SPAM® are chopped pork shoulder meat with ham meat added, salt, water, sugar, and sodium nitrite. Other varieties in today's SPAM® Family of Products now include the following, and the ingredients may vary slightly on each type:

SPAM® Classic (original)
SPAM® Lite: made with pork and chicken; 33% less calories, 50% less fat
SPAM® Low Sodium: same classic taste; 25% less sodium
SPAM® Hot & Spicy: Tabasco® hot sauce added for "heat"
SPAM® Hickory Smoke Flavored
SPAM® Oven Roasted Turkey: features 100% lean, white turkey meat; halal food permissible under Islamic law
SPAM® Garlic*
SPAM® with Cheese
SPAM® with Bacon
SPAM® with Black Pepper*
SPAM® Golden Honey Grail: special collector's edition in honor of Monty Python's award-winning Broadway musical, SPAMALOT
SPAM® Spread
SPAM® Singles
SPAM® Lite Singles

*Selections vary by region; some are limited production items

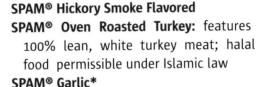

Production

During the last seven decades, SPAM® has been a registered trademark in about 117 countries and is enjoyed by people in even more places. To satisfy the worldwide demand for SPAM®, several plants produce it: two in the United States; and one each in the Philippines, Denmark, and South Korea.

SPAM® Celebrations

There are celebrations of SPAM®, America's favorite luncheon meat, in several locations in the United States, which attract thousands of people. The three known ones are listed below.

Hawai'i's SPAM JAM® is held annually in Waikīkī, where various types of local SPAM™ dishes are featured in the food booths. In addition, vendors sell SPAM® related items from T-shirts to pillows, and local musicians entertain the crowd.

Austin, Texas, hosts its annual SPAMARAMA® Event on April Fool's Day (Note: This is not always on April Fool's Day). This annual festival features a SPAM™ cook-off, sporting activities, and numerous Christian musical acts.

Monterey Bay's annual SPAM JAM® Polynesian Extravaganza is on its way to be coming one of the largest Hawaiian-Polynesian festivals in the country. The two-day festival, held in June, features live entertainment; rides; games; over a hundred arts and crafts and food booths; and of course, SPAM®!

Preparation for Recipes

1. **Slice:** Cut lengthwise into 8 to 10 slices/can.

2. **Chop:** Cut into cubes.

3. **Mince:** Cut into very small pieces.

4. **Grate:** Use large holes of a grater.

5. **Ground:** Use small holes of a grater.

6. **Sticks** or **Strips:** Cut into 8 to 10 lengthwise slices then cut crosswise or lengthwise again, depending upon the length desired. If thicker sticks or strips are desired, initially cut into fewer slices.

7. **Mash:** Use potato masher.

A **can** of any of the SPAM® Family of Products called for in recipes, refers to a 12-ounce can. Unless otherwise stated, **SPAM® with 25% less sodium** is used for the recipes in this book.

Any type of SPAM® may be used for any of the recipes, however, the seasonings may need to be adjusted to your taste.

SPAM™ Classic Recipe

Going back to the beginning, I'd like to share the original Baked SPAM®
recipe which appeared on the familiar blue-and-yellow cans until 1977. It
was also the first of many SPAM™ recipes that I've collected over the years:

1 (12 oz.) can classic SPAM®
    25% Less Sodium or any variety
Whole cloves
⅓ cup packed brown sugar
1 teaspoon water
1 teaspoon prepared mustard
½ teaspoon vinegar

Place SPAM® on rack in shallow baking pan. Score surface and stud with
cloves. In small bowl, combine brown sugar, water, mustard, and vinegar,
stirring until smooth. Brush glaze over SPAM®. Bake 20 minutes at 375°F,
basting often. Cut into slices. Serves 6.

The Secret to Being a Successful Cook

1. Read recipe from beginning to end first. Make sure you understand
   what you're supposed to do.
2. Make certain that you have all the ingredients needed for the
   chosen recipe.
3. Gather all the necessary equipment before you begin.
4. Measure the ingredients accurately.
5. Practice good kitchen and food safety habits.
6. When done, put all the ingredients and equipment away. Wash and dry
   all the dirty dishes and make sure that the kitchen is clean and neat.

Island Favorites

» Hawaiʻi loves SPAM™ musubi. It is great for bento lunches, picnics, and snacks. There are endless variations of this favorite food, and you can also create your own. Here are some recipes that were featured in *What Hawaiʻi Likes To Eat*.

Classic SPAM™ Musubi
Makes 8 musubi

The first SPAM™ musubi I had was made very simply, but I remember it to be sooooo delicious! For those who like simple things, following is the "classic" version.

1 can SPAM®, sliced into 8 lengthwise pieces
4 cups cooked short grain rice
4 sheets nori, cut in half

Fry SPAM® in hot nonstick skillet until browned and a little crisp; set aside. Lay piece of nori flat on work surface and center acrylic SPAM® musubi mold on top of nori. Fill mold with rice and press down firmly. Place SPAM® on top of rice and fold nori over SPAM® and seal. Cool; may be cut in half and wrapped in waxed paper or plastic wrap, if desired.

SPAM™ Teriyaki
Makes 3 to 4 servings

¼ cup soy sauce
¼ cup sugar
¼ cup mirin (sweet rice wine)
2 tablespoons water
1 can SPAM® classic, sliced

Combine soy sauce, sugar, mirin, and water in skillet; bring to a boil. Add SPAM® slices and cook over medium heat 2 to 3 minutes. Drain and serve with hot steamed rice or use as topping for SPAM™ Teriyaki Musubi (see page 12).

10 • SPAM-A-LICIOUS™ Recipes

Tsukudani SPAM™ Musubi

This variation was developed by David Hisashima, a courtroom deputy at U.S. District Court. It's easy to make and really 'ono!

2 cans SPAM®, sliced into 16 lengthwise pieces
1 cup prepared teriyaki sauce, optional
7½ cups cooked short grain rice
8 sheets nori, cut in half
1 bottle (1.5 ounces) furikake
1 bottle (3.3 ounces) tsukudani nori (flavored seaweed paste)

Fry SPAM® in hot nonstick skillet until lightly browned. Brush with teriyaki sauce; set aside. Mix rice with furikake.

Lay a piece of nori flat on work surface. Place SPAM™ musubi mold over center of nori. Fill mold half-way with rice. Spread paste over rice and top with SPAM®. Fill mold with more rice; press down firmly. Remove mold; fold nori over SPAM® and press to seal. Wrap in plastic wrap, if desired.

NOTE:
» Nori paste is available at Asian markets and oriental food sections of markets.

VARIATIONS:
» **Furikake SPAM™ Musubi:** Omit nori paste (tsukudani); proceed as directed.
» **SPAM™ Omelet Musubi:** Scramble 2 to 3 large eggs with 1 teaspoon soy sauce; cook in hot oil in skillet until well done; slice to fit musubi mold. Sprinkle furikake over rice before topping with egg, followed by slice of SPAM®. Fold nori over SPAM® and press to seal.
» **SPAM™ Teriyaki Musubi:** Cook SPAM® slices in ¼ cup each of soy sauce, mirin, and sugar for 1 to 2 minutes. Drain well before placing on rice; fold nori over SPAM® and press to seal.
» **Korean-Style SPAM™ Musubi:** Toss cooked rice with 1 teaspoon toasted sesame seeds and 1 tablespoon sesame-chili oil; mix well. Place well-drained chopped cabbage kim chee (Korean pickle) on rice before placing SPAM® on rice; fold nori over SPAM® and press to seal.

Broiled SPAM™ Nigiri

Makes 24 pieces

4 cups cooked short grain rice, cooled to room temperature
1/3 cup Nori Komi Furikake (sesame seed and seaweed seasoning)
6 dried shiitake mushrooms, soaked in warm water and minced
1 can SPAM®, finely chopped
¾ cup sour cream
½ cup mayonnaise
2 packages (0.19 ounce each) Korean nori (seasoned seaweed)

Spread rice in 9 × 13-inch pan; sprinkle furikake evenly over rice; set aside. Mix together mushrooms, SPAM®, sour cream, and mayonnaise; spread mixture evenly over furikake layer. Broil 5 to 6 minutes or until light brown. Cool; cut into 24 pieces. Wrap each piece in sheet of Korean nori to serve.

SPAM™ Omelet

Makes about 2 servings

1/3 cup minced SPAM®
2 tablespoons chopped onion
1 tablespoon salad oil
2 tablespoons minced green onion
4 eggs, beaten

Stir-fry SPAM® and onion in hot oil in skillet or omelet pan about 30 seconds. Pour eggs and green onion into pan and stir with fork to spread eggs continuously over bottom of pan as they thicken. Let stand over heat a few seconds to brown bottom of omelet lightly. Tilt pan, run fork under edge of omelet, then jerk skillet sharply to loosen eggs from bottom of skillet. Fold portion of omelet just to center; turn omelet onto plate, flipping folded portion of omelet so it rolls over the bottom. Serve with soy sauce or catsup, if desired.

» SPAM™ website is www.SPAM.com

Sam Choy's Pineapple SPAM®

Chef Sam Choy, renowned Island chef and SPAMBASSADOR™, shares this 'onolicious recipe for all to enjoy!

1 can SPAM®, cubed
1 cup pineapple, cubed
½ cup soy sauce
Sliced ginger to taste
1 cup brown sugar
½ cup pineapple juice

Combine all of the ingredients in a saucepan; bring to a boil. Reduce heat to simmer and serve.

Fried SPAM®

1 can SPAM® of choice

MAYO-SOY SAUCE:
½ cup mayonnaise
2 tablespoons soy sauce

Cut SPAM® into 8 slices. Place SPAM® in heated nonstick skillet and pan-fry until of desired crispness on both sides. Drain on absorbent paper. Serve as is over hot steamed rice or with soy sauce or catsup, if desired. SPAM® served on a bed of shredded cabbage and topped with a dollop of Mayo-Soy Sauce is 'ono too!

To prepare Mayo-Soy Sauce, mix mayonnaise and soy sauce together until well blended. More soy sauce may be added, if desired.

SPAM™ Saimin Salad

2 packages (9.5 ounces each) fresh saimin or ramen

SUGGESTED CONDIMENTS:
1 small cucumber, julienne
2 cups bean sprouts, blanched
1 cup SPAM® strips
½ cup minced green onion
Fried egg strips
Teriyaki kizami nori (shredded seaweed)

SAUCE:
⅔ cup water
2½ teaspoons (1 package) dashi-no-moto (fish broth powder)
¾ cup rice vinegar
⅓ cup soy sauce
⅔ cup sugar
¼ cup sesame oil
Hot sauce to taste, optional

Cook saimin as directed on package. Rinse, drain, and chill. Arrange noodles in individual serving bowls; arrange condiments over noodles.

Combine Sauce ingredients in a jar; cover and shake vigorously. Pour over dish of noodles to serve.

> » For accurate measurements, use a set of graduated measuring cups for measuring all dry ingredients. Use a glass measuring cup for liquid ingredients only.

Saimin with SPAM®

Makes about 2 servings

1 package (9.5 ounces) fresh saimin

BROTH:

4 cups water
2½ teaspoons dashi-no-moto (fish broth powder)
¼ cup soy sauce
3 tablespoons mirin (sweet rice wine)

CONDIMENTS:

Fried egg strips
¼ cup SPAM® strips
6 slices kamaboko (fishcake)
Minced green onion
Kizami nori (shredded seaweed)

Cook saimin as directed on package. Rinse and drain. To make Broth, combine water, dashi-no-moto, soy sauce, and mirin; bring to a boil. Place cooked noodles in individual bowls, cover with broth, and sprinkle with desired condiments. Serve with Mustard-Soy Sauce (see page 22).

SPAM® 'n Eggs

Makes 2 servings

1 can SPAM®, cut into 4 lengthwise slices
4 eggs, cooked as desired

Pan-fry SPAM® slices in nonstick skillet until golden brown and crisp on both sides; drain on absorbent paper and set aside. Meanwhile, cook eggs as desired and serve with two scoops of hot steamed rice or hash brown potatoes. 'Ono with soy sauce or catsup over everything!

VARIATION:

» **SPAM™- Loco Moco:** Arrange rice, SPAM®, and eggs in layers; pour your favorite brown gravy over eggs and serve with side of macaroni salad.

SPAMARONI™ Salad

3 cups cooked elbow macaroni, well-drained and chilled
¾ cup chopped SPAM®
½ cup minced onion
¼ cup minced celery
¼ cup minced parsley
1½ cups mayonnaise

Lettuce
Paprika to garnish

Combine all ingredients; toss lightly to blend. Chill 2 to 3 hours. Arrange salad on a bed of lettuce; sprinkle with paprika before serving.

VARIATION:

» **SPAM™-Potato Salad:** Cooked and diced potatoes may be substituted for macaroni; adjust seasonings.

Island SPAM®

This recipe is from Hawai'i's SPAM JAM®, which is held annually in Waikīkī.

1 can SPAM® Classic (12 ounces), cubed
1 chopped onion
1 clove chopped garlic
1½ cups water
1 cup uncooked white rice
1 tablespoon chopped parsley
1 bay leaf, finely crushed
¼ teaspoon pepper
Ground red pepper

In large skillet, lightly brown SPAM®, onion, and garlic. Stir in all remaining ingredients, except red pepper; bring to a boil. Reduce heat and simmer, covered, 15 minutes or until rice is cooked. Sprinkle with red pepper before serving.

Crispy SPAM™ Won Ton

Fried Dumplings

FILLING:

> 1 can SPAM®, finely minced
> ½ pound lean ground pork
> 8 canned water chestnuts, minced
> 4 stalks green onion, chopped
> 1 egg, beaten
> 1 tablespoon soy sauce
> 1 teaspoon sugar
>
> 1 package (50 count) won ton wrappers
> 1 quart canola oil for frying

MUSTARD-SOY SAUCE:

> 2 teaspoons dry mustard
> 2 teaspoons water
> 2 to 3 tablespoons soy sauce

Combine Filling ingredients; toss to mix well. Fill each won ton wrapper with a generous teaspoonful of Filling mixture. Moisten edge of won ton wrapper with water and press firmly together into desired shapes (triangle, rectangle, or fancy). Deep-fry in oil heated to 365°F until golden brown, turning once. Drain on absorbent paper. Serve with Sweet-Sour Sauce (see page 46) or Mustard-Soy Sauce.

To prepare Mustard-Soy Sauce, combine all ingredients and mix until smooth.

> » One hundred million pounds of SPAM® luncheon meat were issued as a lend-lease staple in the rations to American, Russian, and European troops during World War II, fueling the Normandy Invasion.

Dippin' SPAM™ Sticks

1 can SPAM®, cut into sticks or logs
1 egg, beaten
1½ cups dry bread crumbs or panko (Japanese-style bread crumbs)

Dip SPAM® sticks or logs into egg, turning to coat completely. Drop few sticks at a time into crumbs that are placed in plastic bag; shake to coat. Press crumbs onto SPAM® pieces so that they stick; place on greased baking pan. Bake at 400°F for 15 to 20 minutes or until golden brown. Serve with catsup, mustard, barbecue sauce, teriyaki sauce, or salsa as dip. Great as an appetizer, snack, or side dish.

SPAM™-Stuffed Cabbage

12 large cabbage leaves, blanched
1 can SPAM®, minced
½ teaspoon salt
¼ teaspoon pepper
¼ cup bread crumbs
½ cup minced onion
2 cans (8 ounces each) tomato sauce
¼ cup brown sugar, packed
¼ cup vinegar or lemon juice

Combine SPAM®, salt, pepper, bread crumbs, onion, and 1 can tomato sauce; mix well. Place equal portions of SPAM™ mixture in center of each cabbage leaf. Fold ends over, roll up, and fasten with toothpicks; place in large saucepan with cover.

Mix remaining tomato sauce, brown sugar, and vinegar or lemon juice together and pour over cabbage rolls. Cover and cook over low heat for 15 to 20 minutes, basting occasionally. Uncover and cook additional 10 to 20 minutes or until cabbage is tender.

Tropical Baked SPAM®

Makes 4 servings

I remember this recipe as one of the more "fancy" things I learned to prepare while taking home economics in junior high school. In those days, we were not as sophisticated as the teens of today.

1 can SPAM®
¼ cup brown sugar, packed
1 can (8¼ ounces) crushed pineapple
6 to 8 cloves

Cover top and sides of SPAM® with brown sugar and crushed pineapple. Stick cloves into SPAM® loaf and bake at 350°F for 30 to 40 minutes or until brown.

Pineapple and SPAM™ Kabobs

Makes 4 to 6 servings

As a student, I prepared this often for study sessions— it's attractive and simple to make.

1 can SPAM®, cut in bite-size chunks
1 pound fresh marinated mozzarella balls or cheese chunks cut into bite-size pieces
1 can (No. 2) pineapple chunks
Red, green, or yellow bell peppers, cut into bite-size pieces
Bamboo skewers

Thread SPAM®, mozzarella cheese, pineapple, and peppers onto skewers. Brush with pineapple syrup or cheese marinade; cover and refrigerate up to 6 hours or serve immediately. To serve, stick skewers into pineapple shell.

RECIPE TIP:
» Best served cold as cheese will melt if heated.

Mac 'n Cheese with SPAM®

This tops the list for lunch or a heavy snack for my grandchildren. Add 1 cup of frozen veggies to make this a meal-in-one!

1 box (7¼ ounces) macaroni and cheese
½ can SPAM®, cubed
Grated cheddar cheese, optional

Prepare macaroni and cheese according to package directions. Place mixture in casserole; add SPAM® and sprinkle top with additional cheddar cheese, if desired. Bake at 350°F for 25 to 30 minutes or until top is golden brown.

SPAMBALAYA™

2 tablespoons butter
½ pound pork, cut into ½ -inch cubes
1 onion, chopped
1 clove garlic, minced
¼ pound ham, diced
1 can SPAM®, diced
1 bay leaf
1 sprig parsley
1 sprig thyme
1 whole clove
1½ quarts beef broth
½ teaspoon liquid hot sauce
½ teaspoon salt
1 cup uncooked rice, washed and drained

Melt butter in heavy iron pot or Dutch oven. Add pork, onion, garlic, and ham; brown slowly, stirring frequently. Add SPAM®, bay leaf, parsley, thyme, and clove; cook 5 minutes. Add broth, hot sauce, and salt; bring mixture to boil. Add rice; cover and simmer gently for 30 minutes or until rice is cooked and tender. Stir often to mix well. Adjust seasoning if necessary.

Broke Da Mouth SPAM™ Stew Makes 6 to 8 servings

I remember this favorite concoction of some of the
Hawai'i students living in dorms during the fifties.

3 cans SPAM®, cut into large cubes
½ cup flour
¼ cup salad oil
2 medium onions, wedged
5 cups water
2 bay leaves
1½ teaspoons salt
¼ teaspoon pepper
2 cans (8 ounces each) tomato sauce
4 small carrots, cut into 1-inch pieces
4 small potatoes, pared and quartered
1 cup sliced celery

Dredge SPAM® in flour; brown lightly on all sides in hot oil. Add onions
and brown lightly. Add water and bay leaves; simmer 10 to 15 minutes
over medium heat. Add remaining ingredients; simmer additional 20 to
25 minutes or until vegetables are done. Adjust taste as necessary.

Creamy SPAM™ Slaw Makes 4 to 6 servings

1 cup dairy sour cream
¼ cup cider vinegar
1 teaspoon salt
¼ teaspoon white pepper
¼ cup sugar
1 quart chopped, crisp cabbage
½ cup chopped SPAM®
Paprika

Combine sour cream, vinegar, salt, pepper, and sugar; mix thoroughly.
Toss cabbage and SPAM® together; pour sour cream mixture over and
toss gently. Serve on bed of lettuce; garnish with sprinkle of paprika.

Baked Beans and SPAM®
Makes 4 to 6 servings

This is an old-time favorite. A recipe for this dish
first appeared in print before World War II.

⅓ cup minced onion
2 tablespoons butter or margarine
1 can SPAM®, cubed
1 can (1 pound 15 ounces) pork and beans
⅓ cup catsup
1 teaspoon dry mustard
⅓ cup brown sugar, packed

Sauté onion in butter until tender. Combine with remaining ingredients
in a greased 2-quart casserole. Bake at 350°F, for 30 to 45 minutes or
until heated through thoroughly.

Sloppy SPAMMIES™
Makes 4 to 6 servings

1 can SPAM®, cut into small cubes
1 cup chopped onion
1 package (1½ ounces) Sloppy Joe seasoning mix
1 can (8 ounces) tomato sauce
1 cup water
¼ cup chopped green pepper
4 hamburger buns, split
1 cup grated cheddar cheese

Sauté SPAM® with onion 1 minute in nonstick saucepan. Add seasoning mix,
tomato sauce, water, and green pepper; bring to a boil; cover and simmer
10 minutes over low heat. Uncover and simmer additional 5 minutes. Pour
on hamburger buns; sprinkle with cheese just before serving.

> » Tip lids open on casseroles and saucepans from the side farthest
> from you first to allow the steam to escape away from you rather
> than in your face. Steam can cause serious burns.

SPAM® 'n Corn Chowder
Makes 4 to 6 servings

¼ pound bacon, sliced
1 medium onion, chopped
½ cup chopped celery
2 tablespoons flour
1 quart milk
Dash pepper
1 can (17 ounces) cream-style corn
1 can (16 ounces) tiny whole potatoes, drained and diced
1 can SPAM®, diced
Chopped fresh parsley
Paprika

Sauté bacon with onion and celery in 3-quart saucepan about 2 minutes; remove from heat. Stir in flour; set aside.

Stir in milk; heat to boiling, stirring constantly. Stir in pepper, corn, and potatoes. Heat. Stir in SPAM®. Sprinkle each serving with parsley and paprika.

SPAM™ Dip
Makes about 6 servings

2 cans SPAM®, mashed
1 cup mayonnaise
1 clove garlic, minced
¼ teaspoon pepper
Liquid hot sauce to taste
1 loaf round bread (dark rye preferred), center hollowed out
½ cup minced green onion
Paprika

Mix together SPAM®, mayonnaise, garlic, pepper, and hot sauce. Chill 2 to 3 hours. To serve, pour dip into hollowed-out bread loaf; top with green onion and dash of paprika. May be served with squares or rounds of toast for dipping.

All-American Favorites • 31

SPAM™-Stuffed Baked Potatoes Makes 4 servings

 4 medium baking potatoes
 ½ cup milk, scalded
 ¼ cup butter
 ½ teaspoon salt
 ¼ cup grated onion
 1 can SPAM®, shredded
 Grated cheddar cheese

Bake potatoes at 450°F for 1 hour or until tender. Remove from the oven and let cool. Cut potatoes in half lengthwise; scoop flesh into bowl; save skins. Add milk, butter, salt, and onion to potato flesh; beat with hand mixer until creamy. Fold in SPAM®; spoon mixture into potato skins and top with grated cheese. Place stuffed potatoes in baking pan and bake at 400°F for 15 to 20 minutes or until heated through.

SPAM® and Spinach Dip Makes about 4 to 6 servings

An especially good dip when used in Spinach Rolls,
which happen to be a very popular pūpū item.

 1 can SPAM®, minced
 ¼ teaspoon sesame oil
 1 box frozen chopped spinach, thawed and drained
 1 package vegetable soup mix
 1 cup mayonnaise
 1 pint sour cream

Sauté SPAM® in sesame oil; cool and blend together with remaining ingredients. Chill 2 to 3 hours and serve with crudités or sticks of cheese.

VARIATION:

» **SPAM™-Spinach Rolls**: Mix in ¼ cup bacon bits to dip mix; spread on 10-inch flour tortilla and roll like for jelly roll. Refrigerate 2 to 3 hours; slice each roll into 8 pieces; arrange cut side up to serve.

SPAM® Spread

1 can SPAM®, grated
½ cup mayonnaise
¼ cup finely minced celery
⅓ cup finely minced green onion
¼ cup finely minced onion
1 tablespoon horseradish
Liquid hot sauce to taste

Mix together all ingredients; chill 2 to 3 hours. Serve as a spread on crackers or toast.

Grilled SPAM™ Steaks

2 cans SPAM®, sliced into 6 steaks
¼ cup red wine or guava juice
½ cup guava jelly
1 tablespoon Dijon mustard

Char-grill SPAM® steaks. Baste with mixture of wine or guava juice with guava jelly and mustard heated in saucepan. Serve steaks drizzled with remaining sauce.

SPAM™ Home Fries

1 can SPAM®, finely minced
2 tablespoons vegetable oil
6 medium potatoes, cooked and sliced
Salt and pepper to taste

Stir-fry SPAM® in hot oil 10 seconds; add potatoes and season to taste; cook until potatoes are golden brown. Serve with eggs cooked as desired. Great for breakfast!

Great for lunch or as a snack, these bundles are filled with savory chunks of SPAM®, onions, and mushrooms. Best of all, they're easy to make but look so impressive.

½ cup chopped onion
1 carton (8 ounces) fresh mushrooms, sliced
¼ cup bulk pork sausage
1 egg, separated
2 cups chopped SPAM®
¼ cup chopped green onion
Dough for 18 dinner rolls, thawed but still cold

Sauté onion, mushrooms, and sausage until sausage is light brown; place mixture in large bowl. Add egg yolk, SPAM®, and green onion; mix well and set aside.

Combine dough for 3 rolls and roll into 8-inch circle. Repeat with remaining dough. Divide SPAM® mixture equally between the 6 circles and place in center of circles. Moisten edges of dough with water; lift two edges of dough and fold over SPAM® mixture. Lift opposite edges to completely enclose; pinch seams to seal. Place folded side down on a greased baking sheet. Brush with beaten egg white. Cover with plastic wrap and let rise 15 minutes. Remove wrap and bake at 350°F for 30 to 35 minutes or until golden brown.

> » Eggs separate best when cold and egg whites kept at room temperature beat up to their maximum volume.

SPAMWICH™ Sandwiches

1 can SPAM®
8 slices bread of choice (whole wheat, 7-grain, etc.)
Mayonnaise
Catsup, optional

SUGGESTED CONDIMENTS:
Alfalfa sprouts
Lettuce, washed and drained
Tomato slices
Green pepper slices
Sweet onion slices

Cut SPAM® into eight ¼-inch thick lengthwise slices; pan-fry SPAM® in nonstick skillet 1 to 2 minutes; drain on absorbent paper. (It is not necessary to cook SPAM®; it may be served cold straight from the can.) Spread mayonnaise on one side of bread slices; arrange 2 slices of SPAM® on each slice of bread. Spread catsup or sauce of choice on SPAM®, if desired. Top with lettuce or other condiments, then another slice of bread.

VARIATIONS:
»   **SPAM® 'n Cheese Sandwiches:** Add a slice of cheese (Swiss or cheddar).
»   **Barbecued SPAMWICH™ Sandwiches:** Use purchased barbecue sauce instead of mayonnaise.
»   **SPAM® 'n Egg Sandwiches:** Add egg, cooked as desired, and place on top of SPAM®.
»   **Grilled Cheese 'n SPAM®:** Butter bread slices. Place SPAM® slices on unbuttered side and top with American cheese and another slice of bread; brown on both sides in hot skillet sprayed with butter or oil until brown.
»   **SPAM™ Dagwood Sandwiches:** On a slice of bread, stack a slice of SPAM®, cheese, then lettuce, another slice of bread, SPAM®, then slice of cooked turkey or chicken, lettuce and tomato topped with another slice of bread. Use spread of choice on bread slices.
»   **And More**...Use other types of breads (Hoagie, onion, sesame seed, French, Kaiser, croissant, etc.)

SPAMBURGER® Hamburgers

2 cans SPAM®, finely chopped
½ cup minced onion
¼ cup bread crumbs
1 egg, beaten

SUGGESTED CONDIMENTS:
  Prepared mustard
  Mayonnaise
  Sweet pickle relish
  Sweet onion slices
  Tomato slices
  Lettuce

Combine SPAM®, onion, bread crumbs, and egg; mix well and shape into 1-inch thick patties. Pan-fry in hot skillet sprayed with vegetable oil or broil until browned on both sides. Drain on absorbent paper. Place each patty on split hamburger bun and top with desired condiments.

VARIATIONS:
» **Open-faced Burger:** Cut SPAM® into thick slices, pan fry, and place atop French bread slices.
» **SPAMBURGER® Hamburgers with Cheese:** Top burgers with cheese slices of choice while hot.
» **SPAMBURGER™ Plate Lunch:** Pour prepared brown gravy over burger and serve with hot steamed rice and salad of choice (mo' 'ono with macaroni salad).

Easy SPAM™ Potpie

1 sheet refrigerated pie pastry
1½ cups diced cooked potatoes
1 package (10 ounces) frozen peas and carrots, thawed
1½ cups diced SPAM®
1 can (10¾ ounces) condensed mushroom soup, undiluted
¼ cup water
1 teaspoon Worcestershire sauce
½ teaspoon dried thyme leaves, optional

Bring pie crust to room temperature. Arrange potatoes, vegetables, and SPAM® in a 9-inch deep-dish pie plate or 1½ quart casserole dish. Combine remaining ingredients and pour over SPAM® mixture. Place pie pastry over SPAM® mixture. Flute edges; cut slits in pastry and bake at 400°F for 35 minutes or until hot and crust is golden brown.

SPAM® and Pea Salad

Makes 2 to 4 servings

1 package (16 ounces) frozen peas
½ cup minced SPAM®
¼ cup minced onion
⅓ cup mayonnaise
Salt and pepper to taste

Cook peas according to package directions. Drain well and chill 2 to 4 hours; mix with remaining ingredients and adjust taste as necessary. Serve on a bed of lettuce.

> »   Use lemon juice to remove onion scent from hands.

SPAM™ Hash

1 can SPAM®, chopped
6 small potatoes, cooked and mashed
½ minced onion
1 egg, beaten
Salt and pepper to taste

Combine all ingredients in a bowl; mix well and form into patties. Cook in hot oil in skillet over medium heat until golden brown on both sides. Delicious served for breakfast with eggs and catsup or as a side dish.

SPAM™ Breakfast Bake

6 slices bread, torn into bite-size pieces
½ can SPAM®, cut into bite-size pieces
½ cup shredded cheese (cheddar, Monterey Jack, jalapeño, Swiss, or American)
6 eggs, beaten slightly
1¼ cup milk
Dash pepper

Sprinkle half of bread pieces into bottom of greased 2-quart baking dish. Sprinkle SPAM® and cheese over bread; sprinkle remaining bread cubes over SPAM® and cheese. Beat together eggs, milk, and pepper until well mixed; pour mixture over bread layers. Cover with plastic wrap; chill in refrigerator 2 hours or longer. Remove plastic wrap and bake at 325°F 30 to 35 minutes or until table knife inserted in center of food comes out clean. Cool 10 minutes and cut into squares to serve.

» Do not use cracked or dirty eggs as they may have been contaminated with harmful bacteria.

Minced SPAM™ Lettuce Wrap

Makes about 4 servings

1 can SPAM®, minced
½ teaspoon sugar
1 teaspoon cornstarch
2 teaspoons soy sauce
1 teaspoon mirin (sweet rice wine)
1 tablespoon water
1 teaspoon oil
1 teaspoon minced garlic
1 teaspoon minced fresh ginger
1 teaspoon sesame oil
¼ cup bamboo shoots, minced
3 dried mushrooms, soaked in warm water and chopped
¼ cup carrots, chopped fine

Lettuce leaves
Hoisin sauce

Combine SPAM®, sugar, cornstarch, soy sauce, mirin, and water; mix well and let stand 1 to 2 hours. Using a wok, heat oil and sauté the garlic and ginger; add marinated SPAM® and sauté until golden; remove from wok. Heat sesame oil and stir-fry bamboo shoots, mushrooms, and carrots 1 minute; return SPAM®; toss again and roll mixture in lettuce leaves to serve. Serve with Hoisin sauce as dip.

» SPAM® is sold in forty-one countries as of 2003.

SPAM™ Gau Gee

Meat Dumplings

1 can SPAM®, minced
½ pound shrimp, shelled, cleaned, and minced
2 tablespoons minced green onion
2 tablespoons minced water chestnuts
1 teaspoon fresh ginger juice
¼ teaspoon salt
2 tablespoons soy sauce
1 tablespoon sesame oil
1 tablespoon sherry

1 package (50 count) won ton wrappers
Canola oil for deep frying

SWEET-SOUR SAUCE:
⅓ cup sugar
¼ cup soy sauce
2 tablespoons sherry
2 tablespoons catsup
3 tablespoons vinegar
2 tablespoons cornstarch
1 cup water

Mix together SPAM®, shrimp, green onion, water chestnuts, ginger juice, salt, soy sauce, sesame oil, and sherry in a bowl. Place a generous teaspoonful of mixture in middle of won ton wrapper. Moisten edges of wrapper; fold in half and press edges together to seal with mixture of cornstarch and water. Deep-fry in oil heated to 365°F until golden brown. Drain on absorbent paper and serve hot or at room temperature with Sweet-Sour Sauce, if desired.

Mix Sweet-Sour Sauce ingredients together in a saucepan; bring to a boil. Cook until sauce thickens; cool. Serve as dip with Gau Gee or Won Ton.

SPAM™ Lion's Head

6 dried shiitake mushrooms, soaked and minced
10 fresh water chestnuts, peeled and minced
½ cup minced onion
1 teaspoon grated fresh ginger
1 egg, beaten
1 pound lean ground pork
1 cup minced SPAM®

SEASONINGS:

1 teaspoon sherry
2 tablespoons soy sauce
¼ teaspoon salt
1 teaspoon sugar
1 teaspoon cornstarch

¼ cup canola oil
10 cups shredded cabbage
1 teaspoon salt
½ cup hot water

Combine first 7 ingredients with Seasonings in large bowl; mix thoroughly. Shape into 6 patties and brown both sides in hot oil. Set aside. Arrange shredded cabbage in a large pot; add salt and water. Place meat patties on cabbage; simmer over medium heat for 30 minutes or until patties are cooked through. Serve with steamed rice.

» To reduce odors when cooking cruciferous vegetables such as cabbage and cauliflower, add a little vinegar to the cooking water.

SPAM™ Chow Fun
Stir-Fried Flat Noodles

Makes 6 to 8 servings

2 tablespoons salad oil
1 can SPAM®, slivered
1 small onion, sliced
1 package (12 ounces) bean sprouts
1 small carrot, julienne
½ cup chopped green onion
2 packages (12 ounces each) fresh chow fun noodles, cut into ½-inch strips

SEASONINGS:

2 teaspoons salt
1 teaspoon oyster sauce

GARNISHES:

Chinese parsley
2 slices SPAM®, slivered (optional)

Stir-fry SPAM® in hot oil with vegetables for 1 to 2 minutes. Add noodles, salt, and oyster sauce; stir-fry additional minute or until noodles are heated through. Serve noodles on large platter; garnish with Chinese parsley and additional SPAM®, if desired.

NOTE:

» Chicken or beef broth may be used as gravy, if desired.

SPAM™ Chien Doi
SPAM®-Filled Doughnuts

1½ cups (½ pound) Chinese brown sugar
1¼ cups hot water
3¾ cups (1 pound) no mei fun (mochi flour)
1 teaspoon sherry

FILLING:

1 can SPAM®, finely chopped
2 stalks green onion, minced
1 teaspoon oyster sauce

½ cup sesame seeds
1 quart canola oil for frying

Dissolve brown sugar in hot water; cool. Stir enough liquid into mochi flour to make a stiff dough (do not knead). Add sherry and stir to combine. Shape into a roll, 1½ inches in diameter; cut into ½-inch slices; flatten.

Combine Filling ingredients; mix well. Place about 1 tablespoon in center of dough circle. Pinch edges together to seal; roll into a ball. Roll in sesame seeds. Deep-fry in oil heated to 375°F until golden brown. Press balls against side of pan while frying so balls will expand. Drain on absorbent paper.

> » Use a plastic or acrylic knife to cut mochi to prevent sticking.
> » Seeds and nuts keep best and longest when stored in freezer.

Paper-Wrapped SPAM®

1 pound boneless chicken, slivered
½ can (6 ounces) SPAM®, slivered

CHICKEN MARINADE:
2 tablespoons soy sauce
1 tablespoon salad oil
2 tablespoons sherry
2 teaspoons cornstarch
1 teaspoon sugar
¼ teaspoon pepper
1 teaspoon salt

3 dozen 5-inch squares parchment or waxed paper
1 quart canola oil for frying

Combine Marinade ingredients; marinate chicken for 1 hour. Place chicken and SPAM® in center of parchment/waxed paper. To wrap, fold paper diagonally to within ½-inch of the edge; fold right corner to center, then left corner to center. Fold bottom up so packet looks like envelope; turn top corner of paper down and fit into slit made by folds in paper. Fry in oil heated to 365°F about 30 seconds on each side or until meat showing through paper is golden. Drain on absorbent paper. Serve hot. Delicious pūpū!

> » Use plastic cutting board to cut up raw poultry, meat, or fish. Wash the board with hot soapy water after every use and before using it with another type of food.

SPAM® with Green Beans Stir-Fry

1 can SPAM®, cut into thin logs
1 clove garlic, minced
1 teaspoon oyster sauce
1 teaspoon cornstarch
3 tablespoons salad oil
2 cups green beans, cut into 2-inch lengths
½ cup sliced onion
¼ cup chicken broth
1 egg, slightly beaten

Mix together SPAM®, garlic, oyster sauce, and cornstarch; let stand 30 minutes. Heat 2 tablespoons of oil over high heat in wok; sear SPAM® slices and remove to warm plate. Add remaining tablespoon of oil to wok; stir-fry beans and onion 30 seconds. Add garlic marinade, broth, egg, and SPAM®. Cover and simmer 1 minute or until beans are cooked as desired. Serve hot over steamed rice.

> » Garnish cooked vegetables with toasted sesame seeds, chopped nuts, crumbled cooked bacon, canned French fried onions, or slightly crushed seasoned croutons.

SPAM™ Fried Rice

3 tablespoons salad oil
¼ pound shrimp, cleaned and minced
1¼ cups diced SPAM®
6 cups cold cooked rice

SEASONINGS:

2 tablespoons soy sauce
1 tablespoon oyster sauce
¼ teaspoon salt
2 eggs, beaten

GARNISHES:

½ cup chopped green onion
2 slices SPAM®, slivered

Stir-fry shrimp and SPAM® in hot oil 1 to 2 minutes. Add rice and stir-fry additional 2 minutes or until rice is heated through. Add Seasonings and egg; cook additional minute while mixing and tossing gently until egg is cooked. Garnish with green onion and additional SPAM® to serve.

> » Split and toast English muffins; slather with cheese spread of choice and top with diced SPAM®.

SPAM™ Gon Lo Mein

Makes 4 to 6 servings

Fried Noodles

1 tablespoon salad oil
½ cup boneless chicken, slivered
½ cup char siu, slivered
4 slices SPAM®, slivered
¼ cup bamboo shoots, sliced
½ cup sliced round onion
2 stalks green onion, cut in 1½-inch lengths
½ pound bean sprouts
1 tablespoon toasted sesame seeds
1 pound fresh fried noodles (chow mein)

SEASONINGS:

1 teaspoon oyster sauce
¼ cup chicken broth
1 teaspoon salt
2 tablespoons toasted sesame seeds

GARNISHES:

¼ cup Chinese parsley (cilantro)
2 slices SPAM®, slivered

Stir-fry chicken in hot oil for 1 to 2 minutes. Add char siu and SPAM®, stir-fry additional minutes. Add all remaining ingredients plus Seasonings. Stir-fry additional minute to heat through. Garnish with Chinese parsley and SPAM® to serve.

RECIPE TIP:

» Gon Lo Mein may be baked in the oven instead at 350°F for 15 to 20 minutes or until vegetables are done after all the ingredients, except garnishes, are tossed together in a 9 × 13-inch pan.

SPAM™ Fu Yong
Egg Omelet

4 eggs, well beaten
¾ cup diced SPAM®
2 cups bean sprouts, washed and drained
½ cup minced green onion
½ teaspoon cornstarch
¼ teaspoon salt
¼ teaspoon sugar
Dash of pepper

SAUCE (OPTIONAL):
1 cup chicken broth
¼ teaspoon salt
1 tablespoon cornstarch
2 teaspoons soy sauce

Combine eggs with SPAM®, bean sprouts, green onion, cornstarch, salt, sugar, and pepper. Pan-fry egg mixture in hot oil using about 2 to 3 tablespoons for each omelet Cook 2 to 3 minutes on each side over medium heat until egg is cooked.

To prepare Sauce, combine all ingredients and cook until thick, stirring constantly. Serve SPAM® Fu Yong.

VARIATION:
» Bamboo shoots, water chestnuts, dried mushrooms, celery, and carrots, cut into matchstick-size strips may be added. Stir-fry vegetables about 1 to 2 minutes in hot skillet sprayed with oil; cool slightly and add to egg mixture before frying omelets.

SPAM™ Pot Stickers

¼ pound ground pork
1 can SPAM®, mashed
½ cup finely chopped Chinese (napa) cabbage
¼ cup green onion
1 teaspoon minced fresh ginger
1 clove garlic, minced
1 tablespoon soy sauce
1 tablespoon dry sherry
¼ teaspoon salt
24 round won ton or gyoza wrappers
2 tablespoons vegetable oil
1 cup chicken broth
Soy sauce, rice vinegar, and hot chili oil for dipping

In medium bowl, mix together ground pork, SPAM®, cabbage, green onion, ginger, garlic, soy sauce, sherry, and salt. Place 1 tablespoon filling in center of one wrapper; brush edges of wrapper with cold water. Bring edges of wrapper up to meet in center above filling; pinch and pleat closed. Repeat until all remaining wrappers are filled.

Heat oil in large nonstick skillet until hot; add dumplings, reduce heat to medium, and cook until undersides are browned, about 2 minutes. Add broth; cover tightly; boil until liquid is almost evaporated, about 5 to 8 minutes. Remove cover and continue cooking until liquid is completely evaporated. Serve immediately with guests making their own dipping sauce to taste with soy sauce, rice vinegar, and hot chili oil.

» SPAM® is served with instant noodles and fried eggs in Hong Kong.

SPAM™ Fishcake Fry

1 pound raw Chinese fishcake
⅓ cup minced SPAM®
3 teaspoons cornstarch
2 teaspoons sugar
1 teaspoon mayonnaise
1 egg, slightly beaten
¼ cup chopped green bean
2 tablespoons minced carrots
2 tablespoons chopped water chestnuts
2 cups oil for deep frying

Mix all ingredients together in a large mixing bowl. Drop by tablespoonfuls into oil heated to 375°F until puffy and golden brown on all sides. Drain on absorbent paper and serve hot or at room temperature as pūpū or side dish.

VARIATIONS:

» **Shrimp-SPAM™ Fishcake:** Add ¼ cup diced fresh shrimp to above mixture.

SPAM™ Toast

1 can SPAM®, finely minced or flaked
¼ cup raw Chinese fishcake
6 water chestnuts, finely minced
2 stalks green onion, minced
1 egg, beaten
1 teaspoon mirin (sweet rice wine)
12 slices bread, crust removed
Canola oil for frying

Combine SPAM®, fishcake, water chestnuts, green onion, egg, and mirin; mix well. Spread mixture on bread slices; cut each into fourths. Place slices, SPAM® side down, in oil heated to 365°F until edges begin to brown; turn and continue frying until golden. Drain on absorbent paper. Serve hot or at room temperature.

SPAM™ Siu Mai
Steamed Dumplings

FILLING:

½ pound lean ground pork
¾ cup coarsely grated SPAM®
½ cup raw Chinese fish cake
1 egg, slightly beaten
1 teaspoons sugar
¼ teaspoon salt

24 won ton wrappers
Chinese parsley (cilantro)

Combine Filling ingredients; mix well. Place 1 tablespoon Filling mixture in center of each won ton wrapper. Gather wrapper about Filling and pinch lightly around Filling, leaving the top open. Top each Siu Mai with a leaf of Chinese parsley and place in a waxed paper-lined steamer; steam for about 20 minutes or until cooked through. Serve with Mustard-Soy Sauce (see page 22).

SPAM™ Pancit
Fried Noodles

Makes 4 to 6 servings

1 package (8 ounces) pancit noodles (bijon or rice sticks)
3 tablespoons canola oil
2 cloves garlic, crushed
½ pound lean pork, cut in thin strips
1 piece boneless chicken breast, cut in thin strips
1 cup diced SPAM®
¼ pound shrimp, cleaned, and diced
½ cup chopped onion
1 small carrot, julienne
Salt and pepper to taste

GARNISHES:

½ cup chopped green onion
3 limes, quartered
2 hard-cooked eggs, quartered

DIP:

Fresh lime juice
Soy sauce to taste

Soak noodles in cold water for 30 minutes or until soft. Sauté garlic in oil until lightly browned; remove. Add pork and sauté over medium heat, stirring frequently, 3 to 4 minutes. Add chicken and sauté 2 to 3 minutes. Add SPAM® and shrimp and sauté additional 2 to 3 minutes. Add onion, carrot, and seasonings; cook 1 to 2 minutes.

Drain rice noodles and cut into 4-inch lengths. Add to meat mixture and continue cooking, stirring frequently, until noodles are heated through, about 2 to 3 minutes. Place on large serving platter; sprinkle with green onion and arrange alternate wedges of lime and egg around. Serve hot with lime juice and soy sauce dip.

» To help prevent a greenish ring around the egg yolk, cool immediately in cold running water when eggs are cooked in the shell.

SPAM™ Lumpia
Spring Roll

1 can SPAM®, grated
1 kamaboko, chopped fine
⅓ cup chopped green onion
1 package (12 ounces) bean sprouts, blanched
¼ cup coarsely grated carrot
24 lumpia (spring roll) wrappers
Canola oil for frying

SWEET-SOUR SAUCE:
½ cup white vinegar
½ cup sugar
¼ cup catsup
1 cup water
1 tablespoon cornstarch
2 tablespoons water
Liquid hot sauce to taste, optional

Combine SPAM®, kamaboko, green onion, bean sprouts, and carrot; toss to mix thoroughly. Place 2 to 3 tablespoons of SPAM® mixture in center of each wrapper. Fold bottom corner over filling; tuck in two sides then top like an envelope. Moisten edges to seal. Pan-fry in hot oil until golden brown on all sides. Drain on absorbent paper and serve with Sweet-Sour Sauce.

To prepare Sweet-Sour Sauce, combine vinegar, sugar, catsup, and water in saucepan; bring to a boil. Mix cornstarch and water to make paste; add to hot mixture until of desired consistency; bring to a boil. If desired, add hot sauce just before serving.

SPAM™ Pinacbet
Mixed Vegetables with SPAM®

1 can SPAM®, cut into matchstick pieces
1 clove garlic, crushed
1 small piece fresh ginger, crushed
2 tablespoons canola oil
2 long eggplants, cut into thirds
2 long bittermelons, seeded and cut into thirds
1 cup long beans, cut into thirds
2 stalks green onions, cut into 3-inch lengths
¼ cup dried shrimp
2 medium tomatoes, sliced
4 small okra
½ cup water
2 tablespoons patis (fish sauce)
Salt to taste

Sauté SPAM® with garlic and ginger in hot oil until lightly browned. Add remaining ingredients; cover and simmer 15 to 20 minutes over low heat. Toss vegetables in gently to mix; cook additional 2 to 3 minutes or until vegetables are of desired doneness.

> » The SPAM® Museum, located at 1937 SPAM™ Boulevard, Austin, Minnesota, houses a wealth of SPAM™ knowledge in its 16,500-square-foot facility.

SPAM® and Potato Quiche

Makes 4 to 6 servings

1 unbaked 9-inch pie crust
1 can SPAM®, minced
4 eggs
½ cup milk
2 cups frozen shredded hash brown potatoes, thawed
1 can (4.5 ounces) chopped green chilis, drained (optional)
2 cups (8 ounces) shredded 4-cheese blend

Bake pie crust in 9-inch glass pie pan at 425°F for 7 to 9 minutes or until light golden brown. Meanwhile, stir-fry SPAM® in medium skillet over medium heat 30 seconds; drain. Beat eggs in medium bowl; add milk, potatoes, and chilis; mix well.

Remove partially baked crust from oven; reduce oven temperature to 375°F. Sprinkle crust with 1 cup of the cheese; top with SPAM®, potato mixture, and remaining cheese. Return to oven and bake 40 to 50 minutes or until top is golden brown and knife inserted in center comes out clean. Cover edge of crust with strips of foil after 15 minutes of baking to prevent excessive browning. Let stand 5 minutes before cutting into wedges to serve.

> » Sprinkle salt over spillovers in oven while baking to prevent smoking. When baking is finished, scrape up the spill immediately.

SPAM™ Quiche

2 tablespoons minced green onion
1 tablespoon butter or margarine
4 to 5 thin slices SPAM®
1 cup grated cheese (Swiss or cheddar)
4 eggs
1 cup milk
½ teaspoon salt
8-inch pastry shell

Sauté green onion in butter or margarine. Arrange SPAM® slices on pastry; sprinkle with sautéed onion and cheese. Beat eggs; stir in milk and salt; pour into pastry shell over SPAM®. Bake at 375°F for 30 to 35 minutes or until knife blade inserted in center comes out clean and top is brown. Cool 10 minutes before slicing to serve.

SPAM™ Cheese Pie

1 9-inch unbaked refrigerated pie pastry
1 cup minced SPAM®
1 small green pepper, chopped
2 cups grated Monterey Jack cheese
4 eggs, well beaten
1 cup milk

Place pastry in glass pie pan; prick bottom of pastry and bake at 400°F for 10 minutes or until light brown. Spread SPAM® and green pepper evenly over bottom of partially baked pastry; sprinkle cheese over top. Beat eggs and milk together; pour over cheese. Bake at 350°F for 30 to 40 minutes or until knife inserted in center comes out clean. Let stand 10 minutes before slicing.

Haole SPAM™ Laulau

3 bunches spinach
2 cans SPAM®, cut into 16 slices
1 teaspoons salt
½ teaspoon pepper
6 medium yams
¼ cup butter

Remove stems from spinach, wash, and place one-half of it into 11 ×
15-inch baking pan. Arrange the SPAM® on top and season with salt and
pepper; cover SPAM® with remaining spinach. Peel yams, cut crosswise ¾-
inch thick; arrange on top. Dot with butter; cover tightly with aluminum
foil and bake at 350°F for 45 to 60 minutes or until spinach is done.

Oven Kalua SPAM™

1 can SPAM®
1 ti leaf, washed and rib removed
1 tablespoon liquid smoke
Aluminum foil

Place SPAM® on ti leaves; sprinkle with liquid smoke. Overlap ti leaves to
completely cover the SPAM®; tie securely with string. Wrap and seal in
aluminum foil. Place wrapped SPAM® on rack in shallow roasting pan and
roast at 350°F for 45 to 60 minutes. Slice and serve or shred SPAM® and
let stand in mild brine solution with few drops liquid smoke, if desired.

RECIPE TIP:
» To make Brine Solution, combine 1 tablespoon salt with 2 cups boiling water.

SPAM™ Long Rice

1 bundle (4 ounces) long rice (cellophane noodle)
1 cup shredded SPAM®
1 quart beef or chicken broth
1 small slice fresh ginger root
2 teaspoons salt
¼ teaspoon white pepper
¼ cup chopped green onion

Soak long rice in warm water to cover and let stand 15 to 20 minutes; drain and cut into 4-inch lengths. Set aside.

Combine SPAM®, broth, ginger, salt, and pepper in saucepan with cover; bring to a boil. Add long rice and cook 10 to 15 minutes over low heat; mix in green onion. Serve hot or at room temperature.

Spaghettini with SPAM®

Makes 4 to 6 servings

1 pound spaghettini or angel hair pasta
2 teaspoons minced garlic
½ cup olive oil
2 tablespoons minced cilantro
Crushed red pepper to taste, optional
1 can SPAM®, cut into strips
¼ cup lightly toasted unseasoned dry bread crumbs

Cook spaghettini or angel hair pasta until al dente according to package directions. Drain well and set aside.

Lightly brown garlic in olive oil in large saucepan. Add cilantro and crushed red pepper (if used) and stir; add SPAM® and cook over medium-high heat 1 minute. Toss SPAM® mixture with the pasta; add bread crumbs and toss again and serve immediately with garlic bread.

Skillet SPAM™ Spaghetti

Makes 4 to 6 servings

1 can SPAM®, chopped
1 tablespoon salad oil
⅓ cup chopped onion
⅓ cup chopped green pepper
1 can (No. 303) tomatoes and juice
½ cup catsup
¼ teaspoon salt
¼ teaspoon pepper
1 tablespoon Worcestershire sauce
½ cup water
6 ounces spaghetti, broken into 1-inch pieces

Sauté SPAM® in hot oil in skillet. Add remaining ingredients; mix well. Cover and simmer for 30 to 45 minutes or until spaghetti is cooked, adding more water if necessary. Serve with garlic bread.

SPAM™ Lasagne

Makes 6 to 8 servings

1 can SPAM®, coarsely grated
½ cup chopped onion
1 clove garlic, minced
1 tablespoon salad oil
2 cans (8 ounces each) tomato sauce
1 cup water
¾ teaspoon salt
½ teaspoon oregano
¼ teaspoon pepper
1 teaspoon sugar
1 ounce lasagne noodles, cooked per package directions and drained
2 cups shredded cheddar or American cheese
8 ounces sliced mozzarella cheese

Sauté SPAM®, onion, and garlic in hot oil 1 minute; add tomato sauce water, salt, oregano, pepper, and sugar. Cover and simmer 15 minutes over low heat.

Place half of noodles in bottom of lightly greased 13 × 9-inch baking dish. Spread half of cheddar or American cheese over noodles. Top with half of mozzarella cheese slices and half of the SPAM™ sauce. Repeat layers. Bake at 350°F for about 30 minutes or until cheese melts.

> » When cutting onions hold under cold running water or place briefly in freezer before cutting to avoid tears.

74 • SPAM-A-LICIOUS™ Recipes

SPAM™ Marinara Sauce

2 cans SPAM®, minced
½ cup chopped onion
½ cup grated carrot, optional
1 clove garlic, minced
2 cans (8 ounces each) tomato sauce
1 cup water
¼ teaspoon salt
½ teaspoon oregano
¼ teaspoon garlic salt
1 teaspoon sugar
Dash of pepper

1 package (8 ounces) spaghetti, rigatoni, or penne, cooked per package
directions and drained

Sauté SPAM®, onion, carrot, and garlic in skillet over medium heat; cook until onion is tender; drain off excess fat. Add remaining ingredients, except spaghetti; simmer for 45 to 50 minutes over low heat. Serve sauce over cooked spaghetti or pasta of choice.

Easy SPAM™ Pie

1 10-inch unbaked pastry shell
1 can SPAM®, cubed
¼ pound cheddar cheese, cubed
¼ pound mozzarella cheese, cubed
6 eggs, beaten
¼ cup grated Romano or Parmesan cheese

Place SPAM® and cheeses in unbaked pastry shell. Pour beaten eggs over top; sprinkle with Romano or Parmesan cheese. Bake at 350°F for 30 minutes or until cheese is melted and begins to brown. Let stand 10 minutes before cutting into wedges to serve.

SPAM™ Caesar Salad

Created at Caesar's Bar & Grill in Tijuana, Mexico, Caesar's famous salad has been acclaimed by epicures the world over.

1 clove garlic, crushed
²/₃ cup olive oil
4 quarts romaine lettuce, chilled and torn
1 teaspoon salt
Freshly ground pepper
1 tablespoon Worcestershire sauce
1 egg, coddled 1 minute
¼ cup fresh squeezed lemon juice
2 tablespoons wine vinegar
4 anchovy fillets, chopped (optional)
½ cup grated Parmesan cheese
¾ cup croutons
1 cup SPAM® strips

Add garlic to oil; let stand overnight. Discard garlic. Place romaine in large, chilled salad bowl. Sprinkle with salt, pepper, and Worcestershire sauce. Break coddled egg into middle of salad; pour lemon juice and wine vinegar over egg; toss lightly to mix well. Add remaining ingredients except SPAM®; toss after each addition. Adjust seasonings if necessary. Sprinkle SPAM® strips over greens just before serving. Serve immediately.

> » Wash fresh fruits and vegetables before eating or preparing them.

Cheesy SPAM™ Pie

2 cans SPAM®, chopped
½ cup chopped onion
1 clove garlic, minced
⅓ cup tomato paste
1 cup frozen corn kernels
1 can (14.5 ounces) diced tomatoes with Italian-style herbs, undrained
1 refrigerated pie crust, softened as directed on package
1½ cups shredded cheddar cheese

Stir-fry SPAM®, onion, and garlic over medium heat in 12-inch skillet for 1 minute; discard any drippings. Stir in tomato paste, corn and tomatoes.

Place pie crust in 9-inch glass pie pan and spoon SPAM® mixture into crust-lined pan. Bake at 350°F for 30 to 40 minutes or until crust is golden brown. Sprinkle cheese over top and bake additional 10 to 15 minutes or until cheese is melted and begins to brown. Let stand 10 minutes before cutting into wedges to serve.

SPAM™ Pizza

1 purchased pizza crust
1 can (8 ounces) pizza sauce
1 can (4 ounces) sliced mushrooms, drained
2 cups shredded mozzarella, cheddar, or Monterey Jack cheese
¼ cup grated Parmesan or Romano cheese
1 can SPAM®, chopped

Prepare pizza crust as directed on package. Spread pizza sauce over partially baked crust. Sprinkle with mushrooms, cheese, and SPAM®. Bake at 425°F for 20 minutes or until cheese is melted and pizza is bubbly.

VARIATIONS:
» Add chopped bell peppers
» Add chopped bacon
» Add smoked ham

Sushi Rice

5 cups short grain rice
5¼ cups water

VINEGAR SAUCE:
1 cup rice vinegar
1 cup sugar
¼ cup mirin (sweet rice wine)
1 tablespoon salt

Wash rice and drain. Add water and let water come to a boil; reduce heat to simmer and cook 5 to 8 minutes or until water level is reduced to level of rice. Cook additional 7 to 8 minutes over low heat. Let steam, covered, 10 minutes before transferring to large non-reactive bowl or large shallow container.

Combine Vinegar Sauce ingredients; cook over medium heat until sugar dissolves; cool. Sprinkle half over hot rice and toss gently; add more sauce, if desired. Toss and fan rice to cool quickly. Use Sushi Rice in sushi of choice.

SPAM™ Nori Maki Sushi
Sushi Roll

1 can (12 ounces) SPAM®, cut into ½-inch strips and fried
1 jar tsukudani nori (flavored seaweed paste)
10 cucumber sticks, length of sushi nori
10 sheets sushi nori (seaweed)
1 recipe sushi rice

Place sheet of nori on sudare (bamboo mat) and align with edge nearest you. Using hand moistened with rice vinegar, spread 1 cup sushi rice evenly over 5 × 8-inch area leaving 2 inches nori at far end bare. Using a spoon or knife, spread sushi rice surface with tsukudani nori. Arrange a cucumber stick 1 inch from edge nearest you followed by a SPAM® strip(s). Lift mat with thumbs; keep cucumber and meat in place with fingers, and roll mat over meat and away from you. When mat touches the rice, lift mat and continue to roll as you would for jelly roll. Roll again in mat and apply slight pressure to tighten roll. To serve, cut each roll into 7 or 8 pieces. Arrange sushi slices on platter, cut side up.

Uramaki SPAM™ Sushi
Makes 8 to 10 rolls
Inside-Out Rolled Sushi

1 recipe sushi rice (see page 79)
10 sheets sushi nori
20 pieces SPAM® strips
10 cucumber sticks, length of sushi nori
Mayonnaise
Wasabi paste
Tobiko (flying fish roe)

To roll sushi, place sushi rice on plastic wrap that is cut to the size of the sushi nori sheet or bamboo mat. Place sushi nori on top of rice. Arrange a row each of SPAM®, cucumber, mayonnaise, and wasabi paste about 1½ inches from nearest edge. Lift plastic wrap or mat with thumbs while keeping filling in place with fingers. Bring edge of plastic or mat over filling and roll away from you with palm, being careful not to encase plastic wrap or mat. Apply slight pressure to tighten roll then roll in tobiko. To serve, cut each roll in 7 or 8 pieces and place cut side up on plate. Dip in wasabi-soy sauce, if desired.

SPAM™ Chanpuru
Makes 4 to 6 servings
Stir-Fried SPAM® with Tofu/Bean Sprouts

Chanpuru is very popular in Okinawa and SPAM® is often used to give flavor to this stir-fried dish.

1 block (24 ounces) firm tofu (soy bean curd), broken into bite-size pieces
1 cup diced SPAM®
3 tablespoons canola oil
Salt to taste
1 package (12 ounces) bean sprouts, rinsed and drained
2 stalks green onion, cut in 1½-inch lengths

Drain tofu well. Stir-fry tofu and SPAM® in hot oil 1 minute or until tofu is golden brown. Salt to taste. Just before serving, add bean sprouts and green onions and cook 1 minute. DO NOT OVERCOOK. Serve immediately.

SPAM™ Katsu
Breaded SPAM® Cutlet

1 can SPAM®, sliced into 8 pieces
1 egg, beaten
Panko or fine bread crumbs
Canola oil for frying

KATSU SAUCE:

½ cup catsup
3 tablespoons Worcestershire sauce
Dash pepper
Liquid hot sauce to taste

Coat SPAM® slices with egg; dredge all surfaces in panko or bread crumbs. Pan-fry in hot oil in skillet until golden brown on both sides. Drain on absorbent paper and serve with Katsu Sauce.

To make Katsu Sauce, combine all ingredients; mix well. Serve as dip or drizzle over SPAM® Katsu.

VARIATION:

» **Curried SPAM™ Katsudon**: Place slices of SPAM™ Katsu over hot steamed rice in bowl. Pour prepared packaged curry sauce following directions on package.

> » SPAM® was introduced to the islands in the Pacific during World War II, since fresh meat was difficult to get. Surpluses of SPAM® from the soldiers made their way into local diets.

SPAM™ No Mino Age

SPAM™-Shoestring Potato Fry

1 can SPAM®, sliced into 8 lengthwise slices
1 cup flour
1 or 2 potatoes, peeled, slivered, and soaked in water
Katakuri (potato starch) or cornstarch
2 egg whites, beaten lightly
1 quart canola oil for frying

Cut SPAM® slices into lengthwise halves. Drain slivered potatoes well; pat dry with paper towel. Dredge in katakuri or cornstarch. Dip SPAM® slices in egg white, then coat with potatoes and deep-fry in oil heated to 375°F. If desired, serve with cocktail sauce or catsup. Best served hot as appetizer or side dish.

SPAM™ No Kinpira Gobo

Sautéed Burdock with SPAM®

½ can SPAM®, cut into matchstick strips
2 tablespoons canola oil
3 stalks gobo* (burdock), cleaned, soaked in water, and cut into strips
½ teaspoon salt
¼ cup soy sauce
¼ cup brown sugar, packed
2 tablespoons mirin (sweet rice wine)
Chili pepper flakes, optional

Using a large skillet, stir-fry SPAM® in hot oil 30 seconds. Add gobo and stir-fry additional 2 minutes. Add salt, soy sauce, brown sugar, and mirin and cook over low heat until gobo is tender, about 2 minutes. If desired, add chili pepper flakes. Serve as an appetizer or side dish.

NOTE:

» Gobo (burdock) strips that are ready to cook are available in most Asian markets.

SPAM™ Tofu

1 can SPAM®, cut into logs
1 tablespoon salad oil
3 tablespoons sugar
$\frac{1}{3}$ cup soy sauce
3 tablespoons mirin (sweet rice wine)
1 small round onion, sliced
3 dried mushrooms, soaked in warm water and slivered
1 block tofu (soy bean curd), cut into 1-inch cubes, drained
2 stalks green onion, cut into 1-inch lengths

Stir-fry SPAM® in hot oil. Add sugar, soy sauce, and mirin; bring to a boil. Add onion and mushrooms; cook over low heat 2 to 3 minutes. Add tofu and cook additional 2 minutes or until heated through. Add green onion; bring mixture to a boil. Serve hot with steamed rice.

Kyuri-SPAM™ Namasu
Cucumber-SPAM™ Salad

1 or 2 strips wakame (seaweed)
1 large cucumber, cut in half lengthwise and thinly sliced
1 tablespoon chopped carrots
$\frac{1}{3}$ cup chopped SPAM®

SAUCE:
¼ cup sugar
¼ cup rice vinegar
1 tablespoon lemon juice
Pinch of salt, optional

Wash and soak wakame in warm water for 15 to 20 minutes; remove tough center rib and cut into small pieces; set aside. Sprinkle salt over cucumber slices; let stand 20 minutes; rinse and squeeze out excess liquid. Combine wakame, vegetables, and SPAM® with Sauce ingredients; toss and chill until ready to serve.

SPAM™ Yaki Soba

Fried Noodles

½ cup chopped SPAM®
1 teaspoon salad oil
1 small onion, sliced
2 cups bean sprouts
½ cup carrot, slivered
½ cup green onion, cut into 1½-inch lengths
1 pound fresh ramen or yaki soba (wheat noodles)

SEASONINGS:

2 tablespoons soy sauce
3 tablespoons chicken broth
1 package (2½ teaspoons) dashi-no-moto (fish broth powder)

GARNISHES:

SPAM® strips
2 tablespoons toasted sesame seeds
¼ cup minced green onion or Chinese parsley

Stir-fry SPAM® in hot oil 1 minute. Add vegetables, noodles, and seasonings; stir-fry additional minutes to heat through. Garnish with additional SPAM®, sesame seeds, and green onion or Chinese parsley before serving.

> »   Five billion cans of SPAM® can provide a family of four with three meals a day for 4,566,210 years.

SPAM™ Tempura
Fritters

1 can SPAM®, cut into ¼-inch thick strips
Sweet potato, peeled and julienne slices
Bell peppers, julienne
Green beans, French cut
Round onion slices
1 quart canola oil for deep frying

BATTER:

½ cup flour
½ cup cornstarch
1 egg, beaten
½ cup cold water

TEMPURA SAUCE:

1 cup water
½ teaspoon dashi-no-moto (fish broth powder)
¼ cup mirin (sweet rice wine)
¼ cup soy sauce
1½ tablespoons sugar

To prepare batter, combine flour and cornstarch. Combine egg with cold water separately; stir to mix thoroughly. Add liquid to dry mixture all at once; stir only until flour mixture is moistened. Dip strips of SPAM® with a combination of any of the vegetables into the batter. Deep-fry in oil heated to 365°F until delicately browned. Drain on absorbent paper and serve hot with Tempura Sauce.

Combine all ingredients for Tempura Sauce in saucepan; bring to a boil; cool. If desired, add 1 tablespoon minced green onion or grated daikon just before serving.

Spiny SPAM™ Tempura

½ pound raw seasoned fishcake
½ cup minced SPAM®
½ cup flour
4 ounces somen (thin noodles), broken into ¾-inch lengths
1 quart salad oil for frying

BATTER:

1 egg, slightly beaten
½ cup water
½ cup flour
½ cup cornstarch

Mix together fishcake and SPAM® and form into walnut-size balls. Dredge in flour and set aside. Add egg to water and beat to combine; add to flour and cornstarch mixture; stir until ingredients are blended together. Dip SPAM™ balls in batter; roll in somen. Deep-fry in oil heated to 365°F until golden brown. Drain on absorbent paper and serve hot.

SPAM™ Tofu Tempura

1 block (1 pound) tofu (soy bean curd), mashed and excess water pressed out
¼ cup chopped SPAM®
½ cup minced carrots
⅓ cup minced green onion
¼ cup finely chopped roasted peanuts
⅓ cup finely chopped gobo (burdock root)
2 tablespoons sugar
1½ teaspoons salt
3 eggs, beaten
1 quart canola oil for deep fat frying

Combine tofu with all ingredients, except oil; mix well. Drop by spoonfuls into oil heated to 365°F and fry until golden brown on all sides. Drain on absorbent paper. Delicious hot or at room temperature.

Somen-SPAM™ Salad

½ package (8 ounce size) somen (thin noodles)
1 medium head lettuce, finely shredded
1 cup slivered kamaboko (fishcake)
1 cup thin SPAM® strips
½ cup fried egg strips
½ cup minced green onion
Teriyaki kizami nori (roasted shredded seaweed)

DRESSING:

1 tablespoon toasted sesame seeds
1 tablespoon sugar
½ teaspoon salt
1½ tablespoons salad oil
2 tablespoons rice vinegar
1 tablespoon soy sauce

Cook somen according to package directions. Rinse, drain, and chill 30 minutes. Spread lettuce evenly on large platter. Wrap somen into small bundles and place on top of lettuce. Arrange kamaboko, SPAM®, fried egg strips, and green onion on somen. Sprinkle with nori. Combine Dressing ingredients; mix well and serve with Somen Salad.

> » SPAM® has become popular in Okinawa and is used in the traditional Okinawan dish, Champuru.

Hawaiian Temaki SPAM™ Sushi

Makes 10 rolls

SPAM™ Sushi Hand Roll

5 sheets sushi nori, cut in half
2½ cups sushi rice (see page 79)
Wasabi paste
10 pieces SPAM® strips
10 cucumber strips, cut into 5-inch lengths
Radish sprouts
Soy sauce

Place a sheet of sushi nori in palm of hand and spoon about ¼ cup sushi rice over and spread evenly on nori. Place a streak of wasabi paste along center of rice and lay strips of SPAM®, cucumber, and radish sprouts. Wrap nori around filling, starting at lower end of nori and rolling diagonally into cone shape. Serve with soy sauce, if desired.

Pibium Pahb (Bibium Bab)
Korean Mixed Rice

Makes about 8 servings

>

12 cups hot cooked rice
1 can SPAM™ Kun Koki (see page 97), cut into thin strips
1 package (12 ounces) bean sprouts, washed and drained
1 bunch cooked watercress, cut into 1-inch lengths
1 cup purchased cabbage kim chee, drained and chopped
8 eggs, cooked as desired, optional

SAUCE:

2 tablespoons sauce
2 tablespoons sesame seeds, crushed
1 teaspoon salad oil
1 teaspoon salt
1 teaspoon sugar

Cook bean sprouts and watercress in Sauce for 2 minutes; squeeze out excess liquid and set aside.

RICE SAUCE:

1 tablespoon sesame seed oil
3 tablespoons soy sauce

GARNISHES:

Fried egg strips, optional
Finely minced green onion

In large bowl, combine hot rice with SPAM® strips, seasoned watercress, bean sprouts, and kim chee. Pour Rice Sauce mixture over top of rice and toss gently until all ingredients are blended. Top with cooked egg (if used). Garnish with fried eggs strips and green onion to serve.

> »   The largest consumers of SPAM® after the United States are the United Kingdom and South Korea.

SPAM™ Juhn
Batter Fried SPAM®

> 1 can SPAM®, sliced into 8 pieces
> 1 cup flour
> 4 eggs, beaten
> 1 cup canola oil

Dredge SPAM® in flour, dip into eggs, again in flour and finally in beaten eggs. Pan-fry in hot oil until lightly browned, 1 to 2 minutes on each side. Drain on absorbent paper and serve with Ko Choo Jung Dipping Sauce (Recipe follows).

Ko Choo Jung Dipping Sauce
Korean Hot Dip

> ½ cup soy sauce
> 3 tablespoons toasted sesame seeds
> 3 tablespoons ko choo jung sauce
> ½ cup vinegar
> ½ cup sugar
> 1 tablespoon minced green onion

Combine all ingredients in a jar; cover and shake vigorously. Serve with meat and vegetable dishes.

> » Carrots, celery, green pepper strips, broccoli flowerets, cherry tomatoes, or cucumber rounds are all yummy with dips.

SPAM™ Kun Koki
Barbecued SPAM®

2 cans SPAM®, cut into 16 slices

SAUCE:

3 tablespoons toasted sesame seeds

3 tablespoons salad oil

¼ cup soy sauce

⅓ cup finely chopped onion

¼ cup finely minced green onion

1 clove garlic, crushed

1 slice ginger, slivered

¼ teaspoon pepper

2 teaspoons sugar

Mix together Sauce ingredients; marinate SPAM® slices 30 to 60 minutes. Broil or pan-fry until both sides are browned. Best served hot with steamed rice.

SPAM™ Tacos

Makes 12 tacos

 2 cans SPAM®, shredded or finely minced
 2 teaspoons vegetable oil
 ¼ cup chopped onion
 1 clove garlic, minced
 2 tomatoes, chopped
 ¼ teaspoon black pepper
 1 tablespoon flour
 ½ cup water

TOPPINGS:

 2 cups finely shredded lettuce
 ½ cup shredded cheese
 1 tomato, diced
 ½ cup minced onion
 ½ cup sour cream

 12 corn tortillas
 1 quart canola oil for frying

Prepare tortillas by dipping in hot oil and folding in half, keeping top partially open; drain on absorbent paper and place in oven to keep warm. Sauté SPAM® in oil with onion, garlic, 2 tomatoes, and pepper. Simmer over low heat 25 minutes. Combine flour with ½ cup water to make paste; add to mixture and simmer again for 10 minutes or until mixture is thickened. Fill warm shells with mixture. Top with lettuce, cheese, diced tomatoes, onions, and sour cream.

» Hormel Foods Corporation celebrated the production of its five-billionth can of SPAM® on March 22, 1994.

SPAM™ Taco Salad

1 can SPAM®, shredded or minced
½ cup purchased salsa
¼ teaspoon dried oregano
8 to 10 iceberg or romaine lettuce leaves, torn into bite-size
2 cups tortilla chips
1 cup sour cream, optional
1 cup shredded cheddar cheese
1 tomato, diced

Stir-fry SPAM® over medium heat in nonstick skillet 1 minute; drain on paper towel and return to skillet. Add salsa and oregano; cover and cook over medium heat additional minute. Set aside.

To make salad, layer lettuce and tortilla chips in salad bowl or plate; spoon prepared SPAM™ mixture over followed by sour cream, cheese, and tomato.

SPAM™ Empanadas

Meat Turnovers

1 potato, coarsely grated
3 tablespoons salad oil
1 can SPAM®, finely minced
⅓ cup minced onion
1 jalapeño pepper, seeded and minced
1 tomato, diced
⅓ cup grated Monterey Jack cheese
⅓ cup chopped cilantro
Mun Doo wrappers (round)

Soak grated potato in cold water until ready to use; drain before using. Stir-fry SPAM®, onion, potato, jalapeño pepper, and tomato in hot oil until potato is tender; cool. Add in cheese and cilantro; mix well. Place a generous teaspoonful of SPAM™ mixture in center of each mun doo wrapper. Moisten edges with water and press firmly to seal. Deep-fry in oil heated to 365°F until brown on both sides. Serve with purchased salsa.

SPAM® Chili

1 can SPAM®, coarsely ground
¼ cup minced onion
¼ cup chopped green pepper
2 cans (8 ounces each) tomato sauce
½ teaspoon salt
1 teaspoon sugar
1 tablespoon chili powder
1 can (15½ ounces) small red or kidney beans with liquid

CONDIMENTS:
Minced onions
Grated American cheese

Sauté SPAM®, onion, and green pepper together in non-stick saucepan. Add remaining ingredients; stir and simmer, stirring occasionally, until chili is of desired thickness, about 30 minutes over low heat. Sprinkle condiments over chili to serve. 'Ono with steamed rice or crackers!

VARIATION:
» Cottage cheese and shredded Parmesan cheese may be substituted for cheddar or American cheese.

» A can of SPAM® is held for three days to ensure there's no bloating due to bacteria growth. The defective products are removed immediately.

Breakfast Quesadillas

Makes 5 servings

10 (6- or 8-inch) flour tortillas
2 tablespoons vegetable oil
1½ cups shredded cheddar cheese
1 can SPAM®, shredded
5 eggs, cooked as desired
¾ cup purchased tomato salsa, optional

Lightly brush tortilla with oil or spray large skillet with oil; heat in skillet about 5 seconds. Sprinkle on shredded cheese and SPAM®, then top with egg. Brush another tortilla with oil and place on top of egg; cook 1 minute over low heat; flip quesadilla over and cook additional minute or until heated through and cheese melts. To serve, top each quesadilla with 1 to 2 tablespoons salsa, if desired. Cut into wedges using a pizza wheel or sharp knife.

SPAM™ Burritos

Makes 1 dozen small or 6 large burritos

1 cup chopped onion
1 tablespoon canola oil
1 can SPAM®, chopped
¼ pound lean ground beef
½ cup tomato sauce
1½ teaspoons chili powder
¼ teaspoon garlic powder
¼ teaspoon pepper
¼ teaspoon onion salt
1½ cups grated cheddar cheese
1 dozen small or 6 large flour tortillas

Sauté onion in hot oil until tender; add SPAM® and ground beef; cook until brown. Drain excess fat. Add tomato sauce, chili powder, garlic powder, pepper, and onion salt; simmer, uncovered, for 2 minutes. Set aside.

Heat tortillas on a warm griddle for a few seconds on each side. Place 1 to 2 tablespoons SPAM® mixture down center of each tortilla; sprinkle with cheese. Roll tightly and eat like a sandwich.

SPAMISH™ Rice

¼ cup canola oil
1 cup uncooked rice, washed and drained
1 can SPAM®, minced
¾ cup chopped onion
½ cup chopped green pepper
¼ cup celery
1 can (14 ounces) stewed tomatoes
1 cup water
1¼ teaspoon salt
1 teaspoon chili powder

Heat 2 tablespoons oil in large skillet; add rice and brown lightly, stirring frequently. Add remaining oil, SPAM®, onion, green pepper, and celery; cook until soft. Add remaining ingredients; cover and simmer 20 to 30 minutes over low heat until rice is tender.

RECIPE TIP:

» If rice isn't sufficiently tender, add little more water; cover and continue to cook over low heat until soft.

SPAM™ Enchilada

¾ pound lean ground beef
1 can SPAM®, grated or minced
1 can (16 ounces) tomatoes
1 can (6 ounces) tomato paste
½ cup water
¾ cup chopped onion
1 tablespoon chili powder
1 teaspoon salt
¼ teaspoon pepper
1 package (8 ounces) tortillas
Oil
1 cup shredded cheddar cheese

Brown beef and SPAM® in hot skillet; drain liquid. Add tomatoes, tomato paste, water, onion, and seasonings; simmer 10 minutes over low heat. Fry tortillas in hot oil until softened; drain. Place heaping tablespoonful of SPAM™ sauce and cheese on each tortilla; roll up tightly. Place seam side down in 11¾ × 7½-inch baking dish; top with remaining sauce and cheese. Cover tightly with foil; bake at 375°F for 25 to 30 minutes.

RECIPE TIP:

» Prepare recipe as directed. Cover and refrigerate overnight. Bake at 375°F for 50 minutes.

» SPAM™ 'n Cheese Roll-ups are easily made by spreading 7- to 8-inch tortilla with little mustard. Add a thin slice of SPAM®, slice of Swiss cheese, and ½ cup finely shredded lettuce. Tightly roll up tortilla; microwave on high until warm, about 1 minute.

SPAM® and Cheddar Quesadillas

Makes 4 to 5 servings

MEAT SAUCE:

½ pound lean ground beef
1 can SPAM®, finely minced
1 small onion, chopped
1 clove garlic, minced
2 tablespoons chili powder
Dash cayenne pepper
1 cup tomato sauce

10 (8-inch) flour tortillas
2 tablespoons vegetable oil
1 ½ cups shredded cheddar cheese
2/3 cup tomato salsa
¼ cup sour cream, optional
1 avocado, sliced

In a large skillet, stir-fry ground beef, SPAM®, onion, and garlic over medium-high heat, about 5 minutes. Add chili powder and cayenne; cook 1 minute. Add tomato sauce and cook additional 3 to 5 minutes, stirring frequently, until thickened. Set aside.

Lightly brush tortilla with oil and place on baking sheet. Spread about ¼-cup meat filling over tortilla. Sprinkle on ¼ cup shredded cheese. Brush another tortilla with oil and place on top of filled tortilla. Repeat with remaining tortillas and filling. Bake at 325°F for 6 to 8 minutes or until cheese melts and quesadillas are heated through. To serve, top each quesadilla with 2 tablespoons salsa and 1 tablespoon sour cream, if desired. Arrange avocado slices on top. Using a pizza wheel or sharp knife, cut quesadillas into wedges and serve hot.

Marinated Portuguese SPAM™   Makes 4 to 6 servings

    1 can SPAM®, cut into 16 to 20 strips
    ½ cup canola oil
    ¼ cup lemon juice
    1 clove garlic, minced
    1 teaspoon rosemary, crushed
    ¼ teaspoon oregano, crushed

Combine all the ingredients in a bowl; mix well. Marinate for 1 hour. Char-grill or oven-broil SPAM®. Use marinade to baste while cooking.

Portuguese SPAM™ 'n Beans Soup
Makes 10 to 12 servings

    2 ham shanks
    1 package (12 ounces) Portuguese sausage, cut into ½-inch pieces
    1 quart water
    1 can SPAM®, cut into chunks
    1 can (8 ounces) tomato sauce
    1 large onion, wedged
    2 potatoes, cubed
    1 large carrot, cubed
    1 small cabbage, chopped
    2 cans (15 ounces each) red kidney beans including liquid
    Salt and pepper to taste

Simmer ham shanks and Portuguese sausage in water for 2 hours over low heat. Add remaining ingredients; cook 15 to 20 minutes or until vegetables are cooked, adding more water if necessary. Season with salt and pepper to taste.

> » Serve crisp breadsticks and tossed greens with soup.

Portuguese Sausage 'n SPAM™ Omelet

4 to 6 eggs, well-beaten
¼ cup cooked and minced Portuguese sausage
½ cup minced SPAM®
¼ cup minced onion
2 tablespoons minced green onion
Salt and pepper to taste
¼ cup oil for frying

Combine all ingredients except oil and mix thoroughly. Heat skillet or griddle and brush with oil. Drop egg mixture onto hot griddle in small omelets of 2 to 3 tablespoons each. Fry 1 to 2 minutes on each side over medium heat or until lightly browned and the egg is cooked as desired.

Pad Thai with SPAM®
Fried Noodles

Makes 4 to 6 servings

½ pound rice noodles
¼ cup canola or vegetable oil
1 clove garlic, minced
1 egg, slightly beaten
1 can SPAM®, cut into matchstick pieces
¼ pound boneless chicken, sliced
¼ cup water, optional
3 tablespoons nam pla (fish sauce)
1 tablespoon sugar
1 tablespoon tamarind paste, optional
2 teaspoons vinegar
½ teaspoon chili powder, optional
1 tablespoon paprika
1 cup bean sprouts
¼ cup chopped roasted peanuts
1 stalk green onion, coarsely chopped

GARNISHES:

Dried shrimps	Cilantro
Chopped roasted peanuts	Lime wedges

Soak noodles in warm water for 20 to 30 minutes or until softened; drain and set aside. Heat oil in wok on high heat; sauté garlic 1 minute. Stir in egg, SPAM®, and chicken; stir-fry 1 minute. Reduce heat and add noodles. Add nam pla, sugar, tamarind paste (if using), vinegar, chili powder (if using), and paprika; toss gently to combine. Mix in peanuts, half of bean sprouts, and green onions; stir-fry additional minute. When noodles are tender, transfer to warmed serving dish. Garnish with dried shrimps, peanuts, cilantro, lime wedges, and remaining bean sprouts and green onions.

RECIPE TIP:

» Tamarind trees are common in Hawai'i, recognizable for their long, dark pods. Tamarind paste, an optional ingredient in this recipe, is made from the fruit inside those pods. It's very sour and acidic. Find it in Asian groceries. Tamarind is one of the ingredients in Worcestershire sauce.

SPAM™ Goi Cuon
Summer Rolls

8 sheets bahn trang (rice paper wrappers)

1 cup warm water

4 lettuce leaves, cut in half

2 ounces long rice (vermicelli), cooked

½ cup shredded carrots

1 cup bean sprouts

½ cup mint leaves

8 to 12 pieces of SPAM® strips

1 to 2 stalks green onion, cut into 1-inch lengths

NUOC CHAM SAUCE:

¼ cup sugar

½ cup water

⅓ cup wine vinegar

1 tablespoon nuoc man (fish sauce)

2 teaspoons ground red chili pepper

2 tablespoons shredded carrots

2 tablespoons chopped peanuts

Dip rice paper wrapper into warm water; quickly remove and lay flat on dry towel. Lay a piece of lettuce on the bottom third of the wrapper. Place 1 tablespoon long rice, 1 tablespoon carrots, few pieces of bean sprouts and mint leaves on top of the lettuce. Roll up the wrapper halfway to form a cylinder. Fold left and right sides of wrapper over the filling; arrange 2 pieces of SPAM® with green onions and continue rolling to seal. Keep covered with a damp towel until ready to serve. Serve with Nuoc Cham Sauce.

Mix together all ingredients for Nuoc Cham Sauce; serve as dip with Summer Rolls.

SPAM™ Cha-Gio
Fried Spring Rolls

FILLING:

½ pound lean ground pork

½ cup minced SPAM®

½ cup minced green onion

1 small carrot, julienne

1 cup jicama (chop suey potato), minced

2 teaspoons nuoc man (fish sauce)

¼ teaspoon pepper

1 cup lukewarm water

8 sheets bahn trang (rice paper wrappers)

1 quart vegetable oil for frying

SUGGESTED CONDIMENTS:

Lettuce leaves

Mint leaves

Cucumber slices

Combine all ingredients for Filling; mix well and let stand in refrigerator for 15 to 30 minutes.

Place rice paper on a flat surface; brush with water until pliable. Place about 2 teaspoonfuls of filling near edge of rice paper, then fold rice paper over the filling. Fold right side over then the left side to enclose filling. Continue to roll and seal. Deep-fry in oil heated to 365 to 375°F until golden brown, about 3 to 4 minutes; drain on absorbent paper. Place spring roll in a lettuce leaf topped with mint and cucumber slices. Serve with Nuoc Cham Sauce (see page 114).

SPAM™ Bahn Mi
Vietnamese Sandwich

4 French rolls or croissants, sliced in half lengthwise
1 cup cooked SPAM®, shredded or cut into strips
2 small carrots, julienne
1 small turnip, julienne
1 small cucumber, sliced
1 small sweet onion, thinly sliced
1 bunch cilantro
Mayonnaise, optional
Hot garlic-chili pepper sauce, optional

MARINADE:

⅓ cup rice vinegar
⅓ cup lime juice
6 tablespoons sugar
1½ teaspoons nuoc mam (fish sauce)
1 clove garlic, minced

Mix together Marinade ingredients; add carrots and turnips; marinate 4 to 5 hours. Drain well; set aside.

Spread rolls with mayonnaise, if desired. Fill with SPAM®, then layer with marinated vegetables, slices of cucumber, onion, and a generous amount of cilantro. Add a splash of hot garlic-chili sauce, if desired.

> » The SPAMMOBILE® vehicle, a machine that is part blue steel SPAM® can and part monster truck, travels around the United States and brings free SPAM® samples to all.

III. **Appendices**

Glossary

bahn trang: rice paper wrappers

bao: bun in Chinese

char siu: Chinese sweet roasted pork

chien doi: Chinese doughnut

Chinese parsley: cilantro

chow fun: flat Chinese noodle

daikon: Japanese name for large white radish

dashi-no-moto: Japanese instant soup granules

fish paste: paste made from flesh of bonefish AKA raw fish cake

fried egg strips: fried egg cut into strips

fried egg noodles: Filipino noodles; AKA pansit Canton

furikake nori: seasoned Japanese seaweed mix

ginger: gnarled light brown root indispensable to Asian cooking

gobo: burdock root

gon lo mein: stir-fried chow mein noodles

hoisin sauce: Chinese soybean sauce used for flavoring or as condiment

juhn: Korean term for food cooked in egg batter

kamaboko: steamed fishcake

kim chee: Korean hot, spicy preserved vegetables

ko choo jung: Korean hot sauce

long rice: translucent noodles made from mung beans

lumpia: Filipino spring roll with meat, vegetable, or fruit filling

lumpia wrapper: sheets of rice flour dough

Maui onion: sweet-flavored onion grown on the island of Maui

mirin: sweet Japanese cooking rice wine

namasu: Japanese pickled vegetable dish

nam pla: Thai fish sauce

nori: Japanese name for dried seaweed sheets; AKA laver

nuoc man: Vietnamese fish sauce

oyster sauce: Chinese oyster-flavored sauce

pancit/pansit: Filipino noodle dish

panko: Japanese name for bread crumbs

Portuguese sausage: spicy pork sausage

ramen: saimin noodles

saimin noodles: Japanese name for thin wheat or egg noodles

sake: Japanese rice wine

siu mai: Chinese steamed meat dumplings

somen: fine Japanese wheat flour noodles

soy sauce: seasoning made from roasted corn and steamed soybeans mixed with malt-mold, salt, and water, then fermented

tempura: Japanese fritters

teriyaki: soy-flavored Japanese sauce

wasabi: Japanese name for horseradish

water chestnuts: bulb of an Asian marsh plant

wun tun/won ton: Chinese meat dumplings

Index of Recipes

Index

Notes

Notes

Notes

....

....

....

....

....

....

....

....

....

....

....

....

....

....

....

....

....

....

....

....

....

....

....

....